COUNTRIES

EGYPT

R.L. Van

Big Buddy Books
An Imprint of Abdo Publishing
abdobooks.com

abdobooks.com

Published by Abdo Publishing, a division of ABDO, PO Box 398166, Minneapolis, Minnesota 55439.

Printed in the United States of America, North Mankato, Minnesota
102022
012023

THIS BOOK CONTAINS RECYCLED MATERIALS

Design: Emily O'Malley, Mighty Media, Inc.
Production: Mighty Media, Inc.
Editor: Jessica Rusick
Cover Photograph: Diy13/iStockphoto
Interior Photographs: alexeyrumyantsev/iStockphoto, p. 19; Andrei Kravtsov/iStockphoto, p. 26 (left); antonbelo/iStockphoto, p. 27 (top right); Cosmin Iftode/Shutterstock Images, p. 23; Diy13/iStockphoto, p. 25; Filip Bjorkman/Shutterstock Images, p. 7 (map); flowgraph/iStockphoto, p. 30 (flag); Gargolas/iStockphoto, pp. 6 (middle), 17; Givaga/iStockphoto, p. 6 (top); givaga/Shutterstock Images, p. 6 (bottom); Igor Grochev/Shutterstock Images, p. 29 (top left); Joel Carillet/iStockphoto, p. 13; karayuschij/iStockphoto, p. 27 (bottom); lukulo/iStockphoto, pp. 5 (compass), 7 (compass); MaRabelo/iStockphoto, p. 15; npp_studio/Shutterstock Images, p. 28 (top); Osama Shukir Muhammed Amin/Wikimedia Commons, p. 9; pius99/iStockphoto, p. 26 (right); PRISMA ARCHIVO/Alamy Photo, p. 11; Pyty/Shutterstock Images, p. 5 (map); Tamer Soliman/iStockphoto, p. 30 (currency); TerryJLawrence/iStockphoto, p. 21; Tom Bert/Shutterstock Images, p. 29 (top right); Wikimedia Commons, pp. 27 (top left), 28 (bottom)
Design Elements: Mighty Media, Inc.
Country population and area figures taken from the CIA World Factbook

Library of Congress Control Number: 2022940506

Publisher's Cataloging-in-Publication Data
Names: Van, R.L., author.
Title: Egypt / by R.L. Van
Description: Minneapolis, Minnesota : Abdo Publishing, 2023 | Series: Countries | Includes online resources and index.
Identifiers: ISBN 9781532199592 (lib. bdg.) | ISBN 9781098274795 (ebook)
Subjects: LCSH: Egypt--Juvenile literature. | Africa--Juvenile literature. | Egypt--History--Juvenile literature. | Geography--Juvenile literature.
Classification: DDC 962--dc23

CONTENTS

1

PASSPORT TO EGYPT

Most of Egypt is in Africa. A small part called the Sinai **Peninsula** is in Asia. Egypt has the third-largest population in Africa. More than 107 million people live there.

SAY IT

Sinai
SEYE-neye

WHERE IS EGYPT?

2

IMPORTANT CITIES

Cairo is Egypt's **capital** and largest city. It is a center of culture, transportation, business, and education.

Alexandria is Egypt's second-largest city. It is more than 2,000 years old and is known for its history.

Giza is Egypt's third-largest city. It is a center of entertainment. It is also home to the Pyramids of Giza.

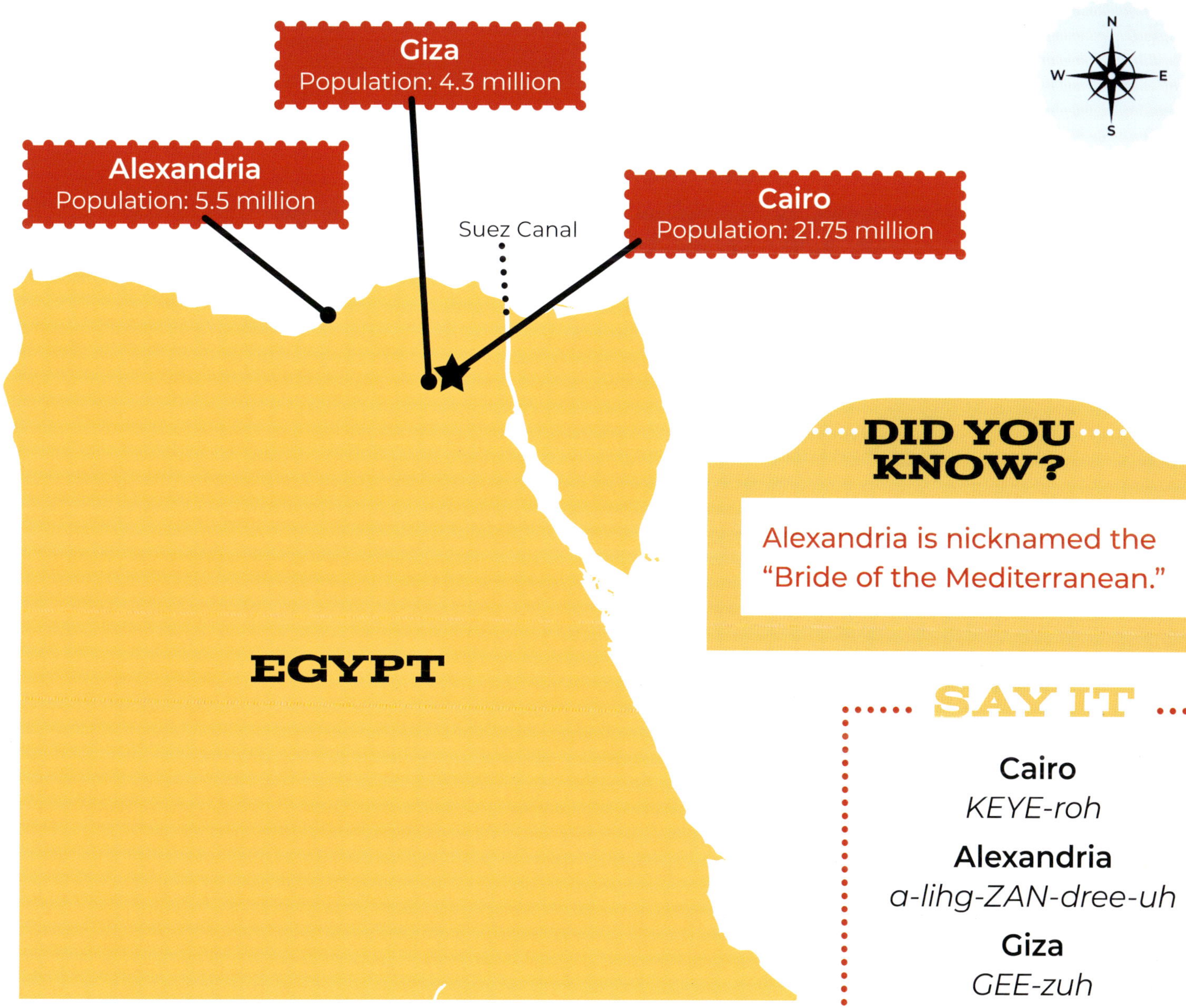

DID YOU KNOW?

Alexandria is nicknamed the "Bride of the Mediterranean."

SAY IT

Cairo
KEYE-roh

Alexandria
a-lihg-ZAN-dree-uh

Giza
GEE-zuh

3

EGYPT IN HISTORY

Egypt was one of the first **civilizations**. It was ruled by **pharaohs** for 3,000 years. Ancient Egyptians made advancements in science, building, and more. Around 640, Egypt became part of the **Islamic** Empire.

Pharaoh Seti I ruled Egypt from around 1290 BCE to 1279 BCE.

Outside forces continued to invade Egypt. In the late 1800s, Egypt was controlled by the British. In 1922, the country gained independence.

Egypt's government became a **republic** in 1953. However, many people still don't have a say. Leaders often punish people for speaking against the government.

The British invaded Egypt during the Anglo-Egyptian War in 1882.

4

AN IMPORTANT SYMBOL

Egypt's flag has red, white, and black stripes. The Eagle of Saladin is in the center. It stands for Arab **unity** and strength.

The president of Egypt is head of state. The prime minister is head of government. Laws are made by the House of Representatives.

Egypt's current flag was adopted in 1984.

5

ACROSS THE LAND

Deserts cover more than half of Egypt. The Nile River flows through the country and into the Mediterranean Sea.

Egypt has ibexes, **jerboas**, and snakes and lizards. Palm and acacia trees, grasses, lotuses, and many other plants grow there.

Fish and crocodiles can be found in the Nile River.

6

EARNING A LIVING

The government controls many Egyptian businesses. Factory workers make medicines, food, and cloth. Many people have service jobs.

Egypt's **resources** include oil and gold. Farmers grow cotton, corn, rice, and citrus fruits. They raise sheep, cattle, and goats for meat.

Livestock have been important to the Egyptian economy since ancient times.

7

LIFE IN EGYPT

Egyptian meals often include vegetables, **legumes**, fruits, and breads. Falafel and figs are popular. Coffee and tea are common drinks.

Egyptians often shop in large street markets. Soccer and **squash** are popular sports. Most Egyptians practice **Islam**.

Street markets in Egypt are called *souks*.

DID YOU KNOW?

About 95 percent of Egyptians live on or near the Nile River.

8

FAMOUS FACES

Cleopatra was a well-known queen of Egypt. She lived from 69 to 30 BCE. Cleopatra was known for her intelligence, power, and charm. She married Roman ruler Mark Antony. They joined to keep their kingdoms safe and strong.

The Temple of Hathor features Cleopatra (*left*) and her son (*right*) on its south wall.

Athlete Mohamed Salah was born in Basyoun, Egypt. He is considered one of the world's best soccer players. In 2012, he began playing for professional teams in Europe. He plays for Liverpool, England, and for Egypt's national team.

Mohamed Salah won the Champions League with Liverpool in 2019.

9

A GREAT COUNTRY

Egypt is known for its history and friendly people. The people and places of Egypt help make the world a more interesting place.

The Bedouins are a nomadic people in Egypt. Many use camels to travel the country's deserts.

TOUR BOOK

If you ever visit Egypt, here are some places to go and things to do!

EAT

Visit a street market to try *ful medames*, a bean stew often considered the national dish of Egypt.

SEE

Take a camel ride to see the Great Pyramid of Giza and the Great Sphinx.

LEARN

Wander Cairo's museums to see mummies, treasures from King Tut's tomb, and more.

BOAT

Take a cruise on the Nile and spot landmarks along the way.

EXPLORE

Visit the Valley of the Queens, where **pharaohs** and other royalty were buried.

TIMELINE

ABOUT 2500 BCE

Ancient Egyptians built the Great Pyramid of Giza.

ABOUT 1340 BCE

Sculptor Thutmose made a famous bust of Egyptian queen Nefertiti. Her face looks very real, which is unusual for art from that time.

51 BCE–30 BCE

Queen Cleopatra ruled Egypt.

1869

The Suez Canal was completed, connecting the Mediterranean Sea and Red Sea.

2011

Mass protests brought down President Hosni Mubarak, who had been in power for almost 30 years.

1171 CE

Saladin became Egypt's ruler. He brought the Sunni **Islam** religion back.

1922

King Tut's tomb was located. Almost all tombs found before this had been looted by grave robbers. But Tut's tomb was filled with gold and art.

EGYPT UP CLOSE

Official Name
Arab Republic of Egypt

Flag

Population
107,770,524 (2022 est.)
15th-most-populated country

Total Area
386,662 square miles
(1,001,450 sq km)
30th-largest country

Official Language
Arabic

Capital
Cairo

Currency
Egyptian pound

Form of Government
Presidential republic

National Anthem
“Bilady, Bilady,
Bilady”
(“My Homeland,
My Homeland,
My Homeland”)

GLOSSARY

capital—a city where government leaders meet.

civilization—a well-organized and advanced society.

Islam—a religion based on a belief in Allah as God and Muhammad as his prophet. Something related to Islam is Islamic.

jerboa—a small hopping rodent that lives in deserts.

legume—a type of plant that bears pods, including peas, beans, and peanuts.

peninsula—land that sticks out into water and is connected to a larger piece of land.

pharaoh (FAIR-oh)—a ruler of ancient Egypt.

republic—a government in which the people choose the leader.

resource—a supply of something useful or valued.

squash—a racket sport played in a four-walled court by hitting a rubber ball off the walls.

unity—being joined together.

ONLINE RESOURCES

Booklinks
NONFICTION NETWORK
FREE! ONLINE NONFICTION RESOURCES

To learn more about Egypt, please visit **abdobooklinks.com** or scan this QR code. These links are routinely monitored and updated to provide the most current information available.

INDEX